Original title:
Into the Mist

Copyright © 2024 Creative Arts Management OÜ
All rights reserved.

Author: Thomas Sinclair
ISBN HARDBACK: 978-9916-90-672-9
ISBN PAPERBACK: 978-9916-90-673-6

The Whispering Haze

In the mist where shadows play,
Voices drift and sway,
Secrets murmur soft and low,
In the twilight's gentle glow.

Through the trees, a sighing breeze,
Carries tales among the leaves,
Hidden truths in hazy light,
Whispers dance before the night.

Echoes of the Hidden

Beneath the moon's soft silver sheen,
Footsteps fade, seldom seen,
Silent paths that twist and wind,
Where lost dreams are intertwined.

In the stillness, shadows creep,
Secrets buried, buried deep,
Memories in the quiet end,
Echoes of what time will bend.

Ambiguities of the Dusklight

Colors blend as day descends,
Lines are blurred, the world pretends,
Fading hues of amber and blue,
What is real, and what is true?

In this space of twilight's kiss,
Shadows dance, a fleeting bliss,
Every moment holds a choice,
In the silence, hear the voice.

Faint Traces of Dawn

Crisp air whispers of the sun,
A new day's promise has begun,
Soft light spills on dew-kissed ground,
Hope emerges, profound and sound.

Birds sing sweetly, a lively tune,
Chasing dreams with the rising moon,
Faint traces of night's embrace,
We welcome dawn with open grace.

Veiled Horizons

Beyond the hills, a mist does rise,
Where secrets dance in twilight skies.
Shadows gather, dreams take flight,
Veiled horizons, lost in night.

Whispers echo, soft and low,
In the twilight, feelings grow.
A journey waits, ancient and grand,
Leading us to a distant land.

Mysterious Threads of Gray

In the weave of life, threads align,
Mysterious gray, a sign divine.
Patterns form, tangled and tight,
Stories woven in the night.

Hands of fate pull with care,
Crafting tales of joy and despair.
Every knot holds a place,
In the fabric of time and space.

Cloaked in Haze

A world obscured, wrapped in gray,
Cloaked in haze, the shadows play.
Figures drift, elusive, light,
Mingling softly, out of sight.

Mystic realms where wishes blur,
Silent echoes, thoughts stir.
In this realm, we softly tread,
On whispered paths, where dreams are fed.

Dance of the Elusive

In the moonlight, spirits swayed,
A dance of shadows, softly played.
Elusive forms, in twilight's grace,
Twirl like whispers in soft embrace.

The night air thick with hidden tales,
As time, too, joins in ancient scales.
A symphony of light and dark,
In every heart, an ember's spark.

Secrets Among the Clouds

Whispers drift on zephyr's breath,
Hidden tales of life and death.
Veiled in mist, the shadows flow,
Stories shared, but few may know.

Dancing light in twilight's hue,
Secrets shared by skies so blue.
In the drift of softest sighs,
Lies the truth where quiet flies.

Journey through the Obscured

Through the fog, the path is frail,
Lost in dreams, I set my sail.
Every step a whisper, soft,
Guided by the visions loft.

In shadow's hold, clarity bends,
A journey started, where it ends.
Every turn, a flickering light,
Leading me through the endless night.

Faint Lights of Dusk

Evening falls with a gentle grace,
Stars awaken, begin their chase.
Faintly glowing, the world transforms,
In tranquil peace, the heart conforms.

Beneath the sky, dreams take flight,
Illuminated by fading light.
Every flicker, a story told,
In the dusk, the night unfolds.

Whispers of the Forgotten

In the silence, echoes call,
Memories linger, before they fall.
Faces fade like autumn leaves,
Yet their whispers in the heart cleave.

Lost in time, their laughter glows,
Carried softly where the wind blows.
Each forgotten tale still thrives,
In the shadows, memory survives.

Silhouettes in the Gloom

Shadows dance on walls, a sight,
Figures twist in gentle light.
Whispers linger, secrets bloom,
Quiet echoes in the gloom.

Flickering candles, soft and bright,
Casting forms that feel so right.
Mysteries wrapped in fabric thin,
Lost in silence, where dreams begin.

Footsteps fade on ancient stone,
Each heartbeat feels so alone.
In this twilight, fears take flight,
Silhouettes fade into night.

Memories flicker, brightly traced,
In the dusk where darkness waits.
Holding on to what we know,
In the night, we fear to go.

Threads of Mystery in the Air

A whisper caught in gentle breeze,
Drifting softly through the trees.
Threads of silver, gleaming bright,
Weaving stories out of light.

Fingers touch the fabric fine,
Echoes linger, intertwine.
In the shadows, secrets spin,
Mysteries woven deep within.

Every sigh, a subtle plea,
Hints of where we long to be.
In the twilight, secrets rise,
Threads of mystery, silent cries.

Navigating paths unseen,
Between the worlds, where we've been.
Lost in thoughts, as shadows sway,
Threads of mystery lead the way.

Dreams Adrift in the Softness

Upon the clouds, where wishes flow,
Where softest dreams begin to grow.
Cotton candy skies above,
Whispers of a gentle love.

Drifting lightly, hearts unwind,
In the stillness, peace we find.
Touched by stars that twinkle bright,
Dreams adrift in endless night.

Floating high on satin waves,
Carried softly, like the braves.
Each imagination takes its flight,
Dreams adrift in soft moonlight.

In the silence, visions weave,
What we seek, we still believe.
Casting hopes on starlit seas,
Dreams adrift upon the breeze.

The Wandering Veil of Time

Time drips slow like morning dew,
Moments lost, yet painted blue.
Veils of memories drape the past,
Whispers echo, shadows cast.

Each tick resonates with grace,
Recollections we can trace.
In the currents, life will flow,
The wandering veil, soft and slow.

Fleeting seconds blur the line,
Between the heart's sweet, fragile sign.
Carried forth on gentle tides,
The wandering veil, where hope abides.

A dance of light, a sigh of night,
Through realms unseen, we take our flight.
Time reveals what hearts do seek,
In the veil of moments, so unique.

The Softness of Uncertainty

In the shadows of doubt, we sway,
Like leaves caught in a gentle breeze.
Questions linger without a say,
Embracing what the heart believes.

Whispers dance on the edge of night,
Promises hidden in your gaze.
Softly guiding, there's no wrong light,
Only paths wrapped in a haze.

Hope pauses, yet time does not wait,
Each heartbeat paints a brand new hue.
Finding comfort in every fate,
As warmth flows through, both tried and true.

With every turn, we learn to trust,
That uncertainty can be our guide.
In the softness, we find our lust,
To seek what in the dark shall bide.

Between the Veils

There lies a world, both near and far,
Where dreams and shadows quietly meet.
Between the veils, a bright new star,
Igniting paths beneath our feet.

Whispers thread through the midnight air,
Secrets linger in the twilight.
A dance of spirits without care,
Traced by the soft, ethereal light.

Moments hang like fragile glass,
Reflecting echoes of the past.
In silence we watch the seasons pass,
As time flows swiftly, ever vast.

A step beyond what we can see,
Is where our hearts begin to soar.
Between the veils, we choose to be,
In harmony forevermore.

Hushed Colors of the Dusk

As daylight wanes, colors blend,
In hues that softly kiss the night.
Whispers of twilight begin to send,
A promise of stars, pure and bright.

Gold and purple meld in the sky,
Painting dreams on a canvas vast.
In the hush, time seems to sigh,
Holding tightly to moments passed.

Gentle breezes weave through the trees,
Carrying secrets of the day.
Every rustle brings memories,
In the twilight, where shadows play.

Hushed colors embrace the calm,
Wrapping the world in a soft hold.
Within this peace, we find a balm,
In the dusk, our stories told.

The Misty Serenade

A serenade drifts through the haze,
Notes suspended in the cool night air.
Misty fingers weave through the maze,
Crafting melodies that softly dare.

Each whisper catches the moon's bright gleam,
Floating lightly on the evening tide.
In the fog, we lose the seam,
Separating dreams from all inside.

Nature hums a tender refrain,
The trees sway to the rhythmic sway.
Through the mist, we embrace the gain,
Of a night's magic in soft array.

With every note, the world feels whole,
Bound by the magic of the night.
The misty serenade claims the soul,
In its warmth, we find our light.

The Ambiguous Line

In twilight's gaze, a line is drawn,
Both lost and found, both dusk and dawn.
It whispers soft like honeyed dreams,
In shadows deep, all is not as it seems.

A path uncertain, where choices wait,
Between the hearts, between the fate.
Each step a question, a riddle to face,
In this fleeting time and space.

Mark it with care, this fragile thread,
Where truth and doubt both tread.
For in the balance, we seek to find,
The pulse of life, the ambiguous line.

Breath of the Enshrouded

Beneath the clouds, a secret sigh,
Carried forth on winds that fly.
Echoed whispers through branches thin,
The breath of those who dwell within.

In shadows cast, their stories blend,
Where dreams take flight, and sorrows mend.
A dance of silence, a gentle tune,
The heart of night, the face of moon.

Veiled in soft and muted grace,
They wander far in endless space.
Each breath a tale, a world unknown,
The enshrouded souls, forever roam.

Enigmatic Wandering

Through misty paths, I roam alone,
In search of places yet unknown.
The echoes call, a siren's plea,
In every turn, a mystery.

With each footfall, secrets unfold,
Whispers of legends, tender yet bold.
A flicker of light, a shadow's guise,
Like fleeting dreams, like painted skies.

The compass spins, the map is lost,
But wandering's worth the heavy cost.
In the heart of night, the stars align,
Leading the way, this path divine.

Clouds of Memory

Softly drifting, clouds above,
Carrying whispers of lost love.
Each puff a tale, each shade a hue,
Of laughter shared and skies of blue.

Beneath their weight, we dream and sigh,
Recalling moments that flutter by.
In silver linings, we find our peace,
Where memories linger, and sorrows cease.

A tapestry formed in the sky's embrace,
Threads of the past, time can't erase.
In clouds of memory, we forever dwell,
In stories woven, we know so well.

Fogbound Reflections

In whispers soft, the fog descends,
A cloak of gray, where silence bends.
Shadows dance on the edge of sight,
Lost in thoughts, embraced by night.

The world is hushed, a tranquil state,
Where time may pause, and dreams await.
Each breath I take, a misty sigh,
In this realm where echoes lie.

Voices linger in the air,
Fleeting moments, unaware.
Reflections wane like distant stars,
In fogbound realms, we heal our scars.

So let us wander, hand in hand,
Within the fog, a timeless land.
For here in stillness, we can see,
The truths that linger, wild and free.

Murmurs of the Unknown

Soft whispers breathe in shadows deep,
Secrets stir where memories sleep.
A quiet voice calls from afar,
Guiding hearts like a distant star.

In every rustle is a tale,
Of journeys ventured, paths grown frail.
The unknown beckons with its song,
In every fear, we find we belong.

Through winding trails, we seek and roam,
Each murmur shapes the heart called home.
With open ears, we learn to hear,
The silent truths that draw us near.

So let us listen, hearts attuned,
To echoes bright, and secrets pruned.
In the unknown, we'll find our way,
Embrace the night, and greet the day.

Treading on Misty Paths

With cautious steps, we tread the mist,
In veils of gray, the world is kissed.
Footprints fade in the cloak of time,
Guided by whispers, soft as rhyme.

Each turn reveals a hidden scene,
A fleeting glimpse of what has been.
The path ahead, a shrouded call,
In misty dreams, we rise, we fall.

The air is thick with stories old,
Of lives once lived, of promises told.
So hand in hand, we wander through,
Seeking solace, finding new.

In every pause, we breathe the air,
Embraced by mystery, rich and rare.
For on misty paths, our spirits roam,
In search of hearts, we find our home.

Hazy Reveries

In twilight's haze, our thoughts take flight,
As day gives way to softening night.
The world blurs into shades of grace,
In hazy dreams, we find our place.

Each pondered thought, a drifting sail,
In gentle currents, we unveil.
With each heartbeat, our wishes weave,
A tapestry of what we believe.

Lost in reveries, we dance and spin,
With every breath, new dreams begin.
Embrace the fog, let go of fear,
In hazy whispers, love draws near.

So let us linger in the dusk,
Where moments twist and worlds will husk.
For in this space, our souls unite,
In hazy reveries, pure and bright.

Shadows in Transition

Shadows stretch in twilight's hue,
They dance as day bids adieu.
Whispers of the night arise,
Beneath the darkening skies.

Fading light, a fleeting glance,
In the dusk, we find our chance.
To wander through the silent air,
With secrets floating everywhere.

The moon awakes, a watchful guide,
Where dreams and shadows softly bide.
Each step taken, moments blend,
In this world where phases mend.

Embrace the night; let spirits soar,
In the shadows, we explore.
Through the mist, our hearts ignite,
In the tapestry of night.

Essence of the Dim

In the corners, shadows cling,
Echoes of forgotten spring.
Dimly lit, a secret space,
Holds the past's embrace and grace.

Flickering lights, a ghostly dance,
Time's essence trapped within a glance.
Unraveled tales, the silence breaks,
In the dark, a longing wakes.

Memories flutter like moths at night,
Drawn to the glow, escaping fright.
In the stillness, whispers sigh,
While the shadows breathe and pry.

Essence lingers, soft and sweet,
In the dim, our souls repeat.
A harmony of dark and light,
Guiding hearts through the twilight.

The Gossamer Horizon

Gossamer threads weave the sky,
Where day and night gently lie.
Colors blend in soft embrace,
A fleeting glimpse of time and space.

Whispers float on the morning breeze,
A dance of light through time's decrees.
Horizons stretch, a canvas wide,
Where dreams and hopes reside.

Feathers of clouds, spun so light,
Cradle the dawn, chase away night.
In this realm where visions soar,
We find the beauty we adore.

Every sunrise brings a chance,
To step beyond, to take the dance.
With hearts aligned, we seek to find,
The gossamer threads that bind.

Murky Pathways

Through murky pathways, shadows creep,
Silent secrets, dark and deep.
Footsteps echo, lost in time,
Hidden truths, a silent rhyme.

Branches reach like bony hands,
Guiding wanderers through forgotten lands.
In the gloom, whispers call,
Seeking solace, we will fall.

Fog enshrouds the winding road,
Where fears and dreams are softly sowed.
Yet in the dark, a flicker glows,
A beacon where the courage grows.

In murk, we find our way anew,
With every step, the past imbues.
Through shadowed roads, our hearts unite,
In the journey from dark to light.

A World Half-Seen

In the shadows, whispers play,
Flickering lights fade away.
Silent dreams weave through the night,
A half-seen world, lost from sight.

Trees stand guard, tall and wise,
Beneath the cloak of unseen skies.
Echoes dance, a ghostly sound,
In the twilight, truths are found.

A flicker of hope, a brief embrace,
Shadows linger, they leave no trace.
In the silence, secrets keep,
A world half-seen, where spirits leap.

With each breath, the night unfolds,
Stories whispered, yet untold.
In this realm, so deeply spun,
A world half-seen, where dreams are won.

The Mist's Gentle Serenade

Veils of gray gracefully drift,
In the stillness, spirits lift.
Cloaked in mystery, soft and light,
The mist sings secrets of the night.

Moonbeams dance on dew-kissed blades,
As shadows play in tranquil glades.
Each note a sigh, subtle and sweet,
A gentle serenade, calm and neat.

Whispers rise like smoke in air,
Cradled softly, without a care.
Every heartbeat feels profound,
In the mist's embrace, we're spellbound.

Through this haze, we start to see,
Nature's voice, in harmony.
The mist's gentle touch, a soft caress,
In every breath, we find our rest.

Lost in the Gossamer Gloom

Beyond the stars, where shadows sigh,
In gossamer gloom, dreams drift and fly.
A tapestry woven of twilight and stars,
Captured in silence, behind the bars.

Whispers float on a silken breeze,
Carrying secrets from midnight trees.
Nostalgia swirls, a delicate dance,
In the dimming light, we take our chance.

Each heartbeat echoes, a fleeting breath,
In the embrace of shadowed death.
Lost in the depths of this silk-spun night,
We wander, entranced by fading light.

But in this darkness, we find our way,
A glimmer of hope to guide our stay.
For in gossamer gloom, we learn to trust,
Even in shadows, there's beauty we must.

Haunting Lullabies of the Fog

Softly it wraps, a blanket of gray,
The fog descends, taking light away.
With haunting tunes that sway and glide,
Lullabies whispered from the tide.

Shadows blend in the soft embrace,
Of nature's song, a gentle grace.
Each note a memory, sweet and long,
Echoing softly, a melancholic song.

In the stillness, hearts align,
As foggy tendrils intertwine.
A haunting lullaby finds its voice,
In the misty night, we rejoice.

Through hidden pathways, dreams take flight,
Guided by the shimmering light.
In fog's embrace, we find our peace,
With haunting lullabies that never cease.

Veils of Whispering Fog

In the early morning light,
Veils of fog begin to rise,
Whispers echo through the night,
Softly masking dawn's surprise.

Shadows linger in the mist,
Secrets hide in swirling gray,
Nature's breath, a fleeting tryst,
Guiding us along the way.

Branches clutch with silken threads,
Gentle fingers, cool and soft,
Sleepy heads on dreams are led,
As the world begins to lift.

Through the veils, we seek the light,
Holding hope in every breath,
In the calm before the flight,
Find the beauty nestled yet.

Shadows Embrace the Dawn

As the night begins to fade,
Shadows dance and softly sigh,
Crimson blush and gold cascade,
Waking dreams beneath the sky.

Warmth awakens, coolness fades,
A symphony of light unfolds,
Whispers of the night's charades,
Wrapped in stories still untold.

With each breath, the day unveils,
All the colors life can bring,
Underneath the whispered trails,
Hearts anew begin to sing.

In the balance, night and day,
Together weaving tales of grace,
Shadows linger, then give way,
To the dawn's bright, sweet embrace.

A Dance with the Unknown

In the twilight's subtle sway,
Mysteries invite the brave,
Footsteps lead us, come what may,
Through the paths of dusk we pave.

Every whisper, every sound,
Holds the promise of delight,
In the dark, new truth is found,
Guided by the stars so bright.

With each spin, the heart expands,
Embracing all the unseen sights,
Weave your dreams with open hands,
Dance beneath the moonlit nights.

In the unknown's gentle keep,
Fear dissolves in twilight's breath,
And the soul begins to leap,
Celebrating life and death.

Shrouded Dreams in Gray

In the quiet shades of gray,
Dreams are woven soft and tight,
Hopes and fears in calm array,
Veiled in stars that guard the night.

With each heartbeat, echoes flow,
Painting thoughts on canvas bare,
Fleeting moments, slow and slow,
Caught between the here and where.

Mystic shadows softly creep,
Cradling dreams that whisper low,
In the silence, secrets seep,
As we linger in the glow.

Shrouded visions start to rise,
Glimmers of what lies ahead,
In the vastness of the skies,
We find the paths our hearts have led.

The Forgotten Path's Embrace

A winding trail through whispering trees,
Leaves falling gently, dancing in the breeze.
Footsteps echo of those who came before,
Their stories linger, forever to explore.

Moss carpets quiet, soft underfoot,
Dappled sunlight on roots that are mute.
Branches arch overhead, a sheltering grace,
Inviting the weary to linger and pace.

With each turn, a memory stirs,
Of laughter, tears, and silent purrs.
A tapestry woven with love and fear,
The path unfolds, drawing ever near.

In the embrace of shadows, wisdom aligns,
The forgotten path speaks in gentle signs.
Amongst ancient stones, time plays its part,
It whispers softly to the wandering heart.

Illusions of a Soft Horizon

The sky melds gold with violet hues,
A promise of dreams nestled in the dew.
Mountains loom like giants, proud and aloof,
Embracing the clouds, tracing nature's proof.

Waves of color flow and entwine,
Painting the canvas where earth meets the divine.
Heartbeats echo in the vast, open air,
Illusions flicker, realities lay bare.

Every sunset whispers a tale to behold,
Of journeys begun and stories retold.
The horizon dances, beckoning to roam,
Finding solace in a space called home.

Yet mysteries linger like secrets untold,
In the softening light, the world feels bold.
We chase the visions that fade with the night,
Surrendering softly to the retreating light.

A Journey Through Mysterious Gray

In shadows deep where silence sprawls,
A journey begins, beckoning calls.
Gray mists surround, a veil so obscure,
Each step forward feels both fierce and pure.

Time stands still, the clocks forget,
Lost in a landscape of dreams unmet.
Whispers of secrets waft through the air,
In the depths of gray, we find despair.

Yet glimmers shine through the murky veil,
Hope twinkling softly, teaching to sail.
Beneath every sorrow, a joy may remain,
In the depths of gray, we find our refrain.

The path lays winding, tangled and bare,
Leading us onward to moments we share.
In the journey through gray, we learn to see,
The beauty in shadows that set our hearts free.

Enchanted by the Blurred Landscape

Fading edges of a world so bright,
Colors entwined, a mesmerizing sight.
The landscape whispers as day becomes night,
Softening visions in ethereal light.

Trees blend with heavens, a canvas alive,
In every heartbeat, the magic will thrive.
Moving clouds embrace the sun's fading glow,
In the blurred landscape, reality slows.

Echoes of laughter weave through the breeze,
Moments suspended among secret trees.
Time drips slowly, as stars start to peer,
In the enchanted realm, all wishes feel near.

Colors cascade in a joyful ballet,
Nature's own art in a grand display.
Spellbound we wander, lost in the dream,
In the blurred landscape, all is as it seems.

Fragments in the Mist

Whispers dance upon the air,
Ghostly forms in soft despair,
Shadows flicker, dreams take flight,
Lost within the shrouded night.

Fading echoes, silent cries,
Scattered thoughts that never rise,
In this haze, I search and find,
Pieces of a fractured mind.

Glimmers of a world once known,
Now in mist, forever blown,
Fragments gather, tales unfold,
Stories waiting to be told.

Yet in the murky depths we see,
Hints of hope, a mystery,
Through the fog, we shall persist,
Holding on to every twist.

Lonely Steps of the Veiled

In the shadows, echoes call,
Lonely footsteps softly fall,
Veiled in silence, dressed in pain,
Wanderers with hearts in chain.

Moonlight flickers, path so dim,
Hope, a whisper on the brim,
Every turn, a ghostly sight,
Lost within the endless night.

Winds that sigh through ancient trees,
Bearing witness to the pleas,
Steps unsteady, hearts in doubt,
Dreams of freedom, fading out.

Yet through despair, a spark ignites,
Guiding souls to distant heights,
Together, in this silence, rise,
Finding strength beneath the skies.

Ethereal Footprints

Softly treading on the shore,
Ethereal footprints, evermore,
Whispers linger in the sand,
Tales of journeys, hand in hand.

With each wave, the memories break,
Echoes of the love we make,
Fleeting moments, lost, they fade,
In the twilight, dreams parade.

Faint the traces where we roamed,
Silent paths, our hearts at home,
Carried onward by the tide,
In this ebb, we shall abide.

Yet as dawn begins to rise,
Footprints vanish from our eyes,
Still, the love will always stay,
In the light of a new day.

The Soft Embrace of Twilight

Beneath the sky, where colors blend,
Twilight whispers, night descends,
Softly woven, dreams take flight,
In the tender arms of night.

Stars awaken, one by one,
Painting shadows, day is done,
Fleeting moments, rich and deep,
In the twilight, secrets keep.

Crickets sing, the world slows down,
Nature dons her velvet gown,
Inhale the magic, feel the grace,
Lost in time, in this embrace.

So let us linger, hearts alight,
In the soft embrace of twilight,
With every breath, a promise made,
In the dusk, our love displayed.

The Enigma of Murky Air

In shadows thick, the whispers cling,
Secrets hide where the nightbirds sing.
Misty breaths weave tales untold,
Underneath the skies so bold.

Figures dance in the quiet gloom,
Carried forth by the scent of bloom.
Questions linger, answers drift,
In this haze, reality shifts.

Faint echoes of a time long passed,
Glimmers of light, uncertain and vast.
What lies beneath this heavy veil?
A story woven, a haunting tale.

Yet through the murk, a glint may shine,
A spark of truth, a hidden sign.
Capture the moment, the fleeting air,
Find the magic that lingers there.

Ghostly Footprints on Damp Ground

Silent whispers in the night,
Echoes fade, out of sight.
Footprints linger on wet earth,
Marking stories of their birth.

Softly treads the shadowed soul,
Guided by a haunting goal.
Each step taken, a tale spun,
In the dance of moonlit fun.

The mist encircles, time stands still,
Filling hearts with ghostly thrill.
Life and death intertwine here,
In the silence, feel the fear.

But warmth remains in the chill,
A pulse, a thrum, a quiet will.
These footprints speak of love and loss,
Whispering echoes that bear the cross.

When Light Meets the Shroud

Veils of darkness thread the day,
As light finds a path, it weaves away.
In the dawn, shadows relent,
Softening edges, a sweet descent.

Glimmers dance on the edges near,
Filling the world with vibrant cheer.
Yet where light kisses the dark,
Lies a realm where dreams embark.

Fleeting moments, the heart does soar,
Mystical whispers from the shore.
Caught between the worlds they tread,
Words unspoken, hopes unsaid.

In this twilight, see the blend,
Where light and shroud do simulate friends.
Every glimpse a chance to find,
What lies hidden in the intertwined.

The Hazy Lure of Twilight

As daylight fades, the colors merge,
A palette rich, an artist's surge.
Twilight whispers, a velvet sigh,
Wrapping dreams as the world grows shy.

Chasing fireflies, the night begins,
Soft serenades and the sweet winds.
In this dim glow, secrets roam,
A gentle tug, calling us home.

The horizon blurs where shadows play,
Inviting hearts to drift away.
Every moment, a lingering grace,
In the twilight's warm embrace.

Yet dawn will break, as it must do,
Carving paths for the morning dew.
So savor this soft, hazy light,
Before it fades into the night.

Echoes in Fog

Whispers drift through the dense gray mist,
Silent stories, each one a twist.
Footsteps fade on the damp, cool ground,
In the haze, lost voices resound.

Shapes emerge like ghosts in the night,
Veiled secrets caught in fading light.
The fog wraps around the weary soul,
Filling the void, making the whole.

Memories blend in the shrouded air,
Past and present in desperate care.
Echoes slip past, soft like a sigh,
In the fog where the lost dreams lie.

Softly, softly, the shadows dance,
In the mist, there lies a chance.
To recover what time has swayed,
In the quiet where echoes played.

Secrets of the Nebula

Stars twinkle in an endless sea,
Whispers of worlds that will never be.
Colors swirl in a cosmic embrace,
Hiding stories in the vastness of space.

Nebulas breathe with ancient light,
Painting the cosmos, a beautiful sight.
Each flicker brings a silent call,
The secrets of the universe enthrall.

Time unravels in celestial streams,
Chasing the shadows of distant dreams.
A tapestry woven with stardust threads,
Where the past and future gently treads.

Galaxies spin in a cosmic dance,
Nothing is random, all has a chance.
In the night sky, answers reside,
To the questions that shadows hide.

Enigma of the Twilight

Twilight falls with a gentle grace,
Casting spells across the face.
Colors blend in a soft embrace,
As day gives night its rightful place.

Mysteries linger in the fading light,
As the dusk steals the day from sight.
A world transformed in gentle hues,
In the twilight, we find our muse.

Stars awaken as the sun dips low,
Secrets unfold in the afterglow.
The air is thick with whispered dreams,
In twilight's charm, nothing's as it seems.

Each moment held in this fleeting time,
A melody rich, a silent rhyme.
In twilight's arms, we chase the dawn,
Embracing the magic before it's gone.

Shadows Caressing the Dawn

Shadows linger as the night departs,
Softly caressing the waking hearts.
Golden rays break the dainty night,
In this moment, all feels right.

Whispers of darkness slip away,
Giving birth to a brand new day.
The world awakes with a gentle yawn,
Embracing the light that greets the dawn.

Birds start singing their joyful tune,
Welcoming warmth from the shy, pale moon.
In the blink of an eye, night fades fast,
Leaving behind the dreams that last.

Hope unfurls with the morning sun,
In the dance of shadows, we are one.
A new beginning lies just ahead,
In the light where the heart is fed.

Glistening Veils of the Unknown

In the darkness, secrets glow,
Veils of mist begin to flow,
Whispers dance among the trees,
Promises carried on the breeze.

Stars above, a distant guide,
Shadows murmur, not to hide,
Every step reveals a tale,
Woven deep in night's soft veil.

Moonlight drapes the silent ground,
In its glow, lost dreams are found,
Fingers trace the hidden paths,
As the night unfolds its wrath.

Glistening threads in silence weave,
A tapestry that helps believe,
Though the unknown wraps so tight,
Hearts will soar, embracing light.

Whispered Words of the Obscured

In the depths where secrets sleep,
Words of old begin to creep,
Gentle echoes fill the night,
Shadows dance in pale moonlight.

Veiled in mystery they call,
Softly floating, one and all,
Voices flicker like the flame,
Holding truths without a name.

Lost in thoughts of what could be,
Whispers weave a tapestry,
Threads of fate that intertwine,
Guiding souls like stars that shine.

Through the haze of doubt and fear,
Whispers linger, always near,
In those words, a spark ignites,
Illuminating hidden sights.

Tides of the Unknown

Waves that crash against the shore,
Carry dreams forevermore,
In their rise and in their fall,
Whispers beckon, nature's call.

Each tide brings a tale to tell,
Of lost loves that once did dwell,
Ebbing softly, time moves slow,
Secrets buried in the flow.

Footprints fade in shifting sands,
As the ocean understands,
Nothing stays, yet all remains,
In the heart, the memory gains.

From the depths, the fears arise,
Yet the stars can mesmerize,
Tides of hope and tides of pain,
In their rhythm, life's refrain.

Ethereal Veil

Hidden realms where shadows blend,
Ethereal veils twist and bend,
Colors swirl in mystic light,
Crafting dreams that take to flight.

Glimmers shine through endless night,
Whispers calling hearts to write,
Stories woven in the air,
Filling all with silent flair.

Softly drifting, time stands still,
In the silence, find your will,
Close your eyes, let visions soar,
Open wide the hidden door.

Through the veil, the spirit glows,
Guiding paths that no one knows,
Trust the journey as it peeks,
In the light, the soul still seeks.

Shimmers of the Arcane

In twilight's grasp, secrets unfold,
Mystic whispers, in shadows bold.
A dance of light, a fleeting glance,
Where ancient spells ignite the chance.

Stars align in the velvet night,
Guiding seekers on paths of light.
With every breath, the magic swells,
In every heart, a tale it tells.

Winds carry lore from ages past,
In their embrace, our dreams are cast.
The arcane spark, ignites the soul,
In shimmers bright, we find our role.

So delve into the mystic's lair,
Unlock the secrets hidden there.
With eyes wide open, cast aside fear,
Embrace the magic, hold it dear.

Shadows of Lost Time

In corners dim where echoes dwell,
Whispers weave a silent spell.
Flickering lights in a ghostly dance,
Bring forth memories, a fleeting chance.

Moments drag like shadows long,
In stillness, beats a heart's own song.
Time slips past like grains of sand,
Lost in twilight, a forgotten land.

Ghostly figures from yesteryears,
Lurk and linger, born of tears.
They laugh and weep in quiet grace,
The shadows of time, a lost embrace.

Yet in the dusk, there's beauty found,
In whispered words that swirl around.
We hold them close, like tender rhymes,
In the haunting shadows of lost time.

The Silken Embrace of Uncertainty

Threads of doubt weave through the night,
In silken folds, they hold the light.
A tapestry of dreams and fear,
Unfolding softly, drawing near.

What lies ahead, a path unknown,
With every choice, our seeds are sown.
We dance on edges, hearts in flight,
In uncertainty, we find our might.

Embraced by dusk, our worries sway,
In the twilight glow, we find our way.
With every breath, let go of chains,
In silken threads, our freedom reigns.

So trust the journey, step by step,
In shadows deep, new dreams are kept.
For in the unknown, we start to see,
The richness found in uncertainty.

Dance of the Unseen

In twilight's grasp, they softly sway,
Whispers in the shadows play.
Ethereal forms in moonlight's glow,
Steps of the quiet, ebb and flow.

Beneath the stars, with hearts alight,
They twirl and spin, a fleeting sight.
In silence wrapped, they dance alone,
Echoes of dreams, the unknown's tone.

With every breath, a secret shared,
Unseen connections, souls laid bare.
Through the mist, their laughter spills,
A ballet soft on haunted hills.

Boundless spirits, lost in grace,
In the dark, they find their place.
For in the void, their spirits gleam,
In the dance, they chase the dream.

LIGHTS AND SHADOWS IN THE FOG

A lantern glows on cobbled streets,
While shadows whisper soft retreats.
Mist envelops the night in shrouds,
Curtains drawn 'gainst wandering crowds.

Figures flicker in the haze,
Caught between the light's soft gaze.
A heartbeat pulsing in the gloom,
Where every echo finds its doom.

Footsteps gentle, secrets blend,
In this realm where dreams suspend.
Desires flicker, hopes awake,
Illuminated paths we take.

In this dance of light and dark,
The fireflies dart, a fleeting spark.
Weaving stories, lost and found,
In the fog, our hearts are bound.

Chills of the Enigmatic

Cold winds weave through the night's embrace,
Fingers trace an unseen face.
Whispers echo, soft and sly,
In the void, the shadows lie.

A glance behind brings icy dread,
Footsteps follow, though none tread.
Beneath the surface, secrets stir,
In silent corners, whispers blur.

Every breath a chilling tale,
Of lost moments, dreams that pale.
In the dark, a ghostly sigh,
Shadows dance, yet none reply.

Mysterious forms that fade away,
In the night, they choose to stay.
Enigmas wrapped in ice and mist,
Forever longing to exist.

Spirals of Silhouettes

Darkened figures twist and weave,
Stories told, yet none believe.
In the quiet, shadows blend,
Whirling forms that never end.

Cascading echoes, lost in time,
A dance of fate, a spectral rhyme.
With every turn, they shift and sway,
Carving paths that drift away.

In the realm of dusk and dawn,
Where silhouettes are gently drawn.
Spirals spin, they circle tight,
In their dance, they chase the light.

Open hearts and silent eyes,
Drawn together, where mystery lies.
In every fold, a story lives,
In silhouettes, the spirit gives.

Beneath a Cloak of Vapor

In the misty dawn, shadows creep,
Whispers of secrets in silence steep.
Veils of grey dance in soft light,
Winds carry tales of the night.

Fog rolls like waves on a silent sea,
Breath of the earth, wild and free.
Mysteries hide in the soft embrace,
While dreams and reality interlace.

Beneath this cloak, visions blend,
A world reshaped where illusions mend.
With every heartbeat, the unknown calls,
Where every moment gently falls.

In this realm where shadows play,
The veil of vapor holds sway.
We wander, lost, yet found anew,
In the tender hush of morning's dew.

In the Heart of the Shifting Shadows

In twilight's grasp, shadows weave,
A tapestry where hearts believe.
Silent echoes from corners dark,
Illuminated by a fleeting spark.

Footsteps linger on cobbled streets,
Haunting whispers of love that meets.
Each turn reveals a hidden lane,
Where secrets linger but never wane.

In the heart of the shifting night,
Hope finds refuge, igniting light.
Stars twinkle in the depths of gloom,
Guiding souls to their destined bloom.

A dance of shadows, fleeting and fleet,
In their embrace, we love and meet.
With every glance, a story waits,
In the heart of shadows, love creates.

Whispers of the Hidden Path

Amidst the trees, a pathway hides,
Where nature's magic gently chides.
Leaves rustle soft in the evening air,
Whispers beckon without a care.

Footprints of wanderers long ago,
Carved in silence, tales overflow.
The path winds on, both narrow and wide,
Inviting the lost to confide.

Murmurs of dreams float on the breeze,
Carried gently through ancient trees.
Secrets of ages in shadows dwell,
Where every turn casts a spell.

Here lies the journey, a sacred rite,
In the whispers that fade with night.
Beneath the moon's soft, watchful glow,
The hidden path leads where hearts can grow.

Caresses from the Floating Shadows

In the dusk where shadows bloom,
They find us here, dispelling gloom.
Fingers of twilight brush the ground,
In their embrace, solace is found.

Glimmers dance on the edge of sight,
Fleeting moments, pure delight.
They wrap around, a gentle shroud,
In silence deep, whispers loud.

The evening hums a soft refrain,
As shadows caress like falling rain.
Each heartbeat feels the tender touch,
Reminders of how we long for such.

So linger here, beneath the sway,
Of floating shadows that guide our way.
In their soft presence, we are free,
Lost in the caress of mystery.

Shadows of the Forgotten

In the twilight where echoes fade,
Whispers of time in silence laid.
Figures linger, lost in the mist,
Forgotten tales that still persist.

Under the canopy of sighs,
Ghostly murmurs, where memory lies.
Flickers of light, then shadows creep,
Secrets buried, their vigil they keep.

Once they danced, now they wane,
Faint reflections of joy and pain.
Footsteps trace a sorrowed path,
In shadows deep, we face the wrath.

A candle's glow, a fleeting spark,
Guides the lost through realms so dark.
Yet in the silence, hope finds a way,
In shadows of night, a brand new day.

Veins of Smoke

In the air, a drifting haze,
Veins of smoke in swirling ways.
Each breath carries tales untold,
Silent stories from the bold.

Through the cracks of dreams, it weaves,
Misty patterns that heart believes.
A dance of shadows, a phantom grace,
Holding secrets in their embrace.

Fleeting moments, like whispers glide,
Through the night, they softly ride.
Embers fade as dawn approaches,
Awakening where stillness broaches.

With each sigh, it curls and breaks,
Crafting forms that time forsakes.
Lost in the ether, shadows roam,
In veins of smoke, we find our home.

A Dance with the Unseen

In twilight's veil, where dreams entwine,
Mysteries pulse like a hidden sign.
Softly swaying in the night air,
A dance begins, subtle yet rare.

Footsteps echo on the edge of sight,
Joined by spirits that blend with light.
Invisible partners, laughter rings,
In the silence, the shadow sings.

Twisting forms behind the veil,
Tales of longing, love, and trail.
Together they whirl, a wisp of grace,
In unison, they find their place.

Fleeting glimpses, a soft embrace,
In shadows fleeting, a timeless chase.
A dance with the unseen, so divine,
In the heart's rhythm, we intertwine.

Gossamer Whispers

In dawn's soft light, whispers grow,
Delicate secrets, gentle and slow.
Gossamer threads of the morning dew,
Weaving tales as if anew.

Each breath carries a tender grace,
Murmurs wrapped in a silken trace.
Voices blend with the rustling leaves,
Nature's song that the heart believes.

A flutter of wings, a sigh in the breeze,
Gossamer dreams that linger and tease.
Chasing shadows, we dance through time,
In ethereal realms, a silent rhyme.

With each moment, the whispers blend,
In a tapestry where beginnings end.
Soft as a feather, light as a sigh,
Gossamer whispers that never die.

Breaths of the Enveloping Ether

In the quiet night's embrace,
Stars whisper secrets above,
The moon holds its silver trace,
Every breath is a sign of love.

Winds carry tales from afar,
Echoes of lost hopes and dreams,
The universe, a guiding star,
Illuminating life's soft beams.

Mysteries in shadows glide,
Dancing in the depths of time,
Where the heart's true thoughts abide,
Each pulse a silent rhyme.

In stillness, let your soul soar,
Through the ether's gentle stream,
Embrace the magic at the core,
Awaken to the timeless dream.

Veiled Realities Await

Behind the curtain, worlds reside,
Hidden from the human gaze,
Mystic realms where spirits glide,
Veiled in an ethereal haze.

Each shadow tells a whispered tale,
Of paths not taken in the light,
Through moonlit woods and misty vale,
They beckon softly, out of sight.

Life's journey twists and turns about,
A dance of fate, unseen yet near,
What dreams may come, we've yet to scout,
Through veils of thoughts we hold dear.

The key lies in the heart's pure glow,
To pierce the shroud that holds us tight,
For in the depths, the truth will show,
Veiled realities ignite our flight.

Veil of Whispers

Softly spoken in the night,
Whispers weave through tangled leaves,
Secrets born of its delight,
Carried on the breeze that cleaves.

Underneath the silver sky,
Voices echo far and wide,
In the silence, let us fly,
Where the dreams and hopes reside.

Glimmers of a bygone age,
Stories wrapped in tender care,
Turn the timeless, fragile page,
Veil of whispers lingers there.

Find the words that spark the flame,
In the hush, let your heart race,
For every thought's a gentle claim,
In the veils of whispered grace.

Shroud of Dreams

Beneath the stars, the night unfolds,
A shroud of dreams in soft embrace,
Within its arms, the heart beholds,
A world where time finds gentle pace.

Caress the visions that will bloom,
In the quiet solitude,
From deep within, dispel the gloom,
For every thought, a fortitude.

The fabric of our hopes is spun,
With threads of light and shadows deep,
Awakened by the rising sun,
In dreams, our souls are free to leap.

So let the night, in silence weave,
A tapestry of whispered schemes,
For in this realm, we dare believe,
The boundless beauty of our dreams.

The Secrets of Silver Haze

In whispers soft, the moonlight glows,
Where shadows dance, and silence flows.
A tapestry of dreams unfurled,
Within the hush, a hidden world.

Beneath the trees, the nightingale sings,
A melody of cherished things.
In silver haze, the stories weave,
Of ancient tales, we dare believe.

The misty morn, it holds its breath,
As secrets spill in gentle depth.
In every sigh, a truth resides,
A journey long where magic hides.

Amidst the stars, with eyes aglow,
We seek the paths that only flow.
Through silver haze, we'll find our way,
In dreams that dance, by night and day.

Beyond the Glistening Veil

A glimmering veil, so soft and bright,
Hides realms untouched by day or night.
We step with care, on threads of fate,
In search of wonders, we await.

The echoes call, from deep within,
Inviting souls to start again.
Beyond the veil, where shadows play,
We find our hearts, they lead the way.

In woven light, our dreams take flight,
A tapestry of pure delight.
Beyond the glistening, secrets lie,
In whispered hopes, we learn to fly.

With every step, the world expands,
As time slips softly through our hands.
Beyond the veil, in realms untold,
We find the magic, bright and bold.

Echoes in the Ethereal

In twilight air, where echoes blend,
A symphony, we call a friend.
Through spectral light, our voices soar,
In ethereal realms, forevermore.

The whispers dance on silken threads,
In dreams and thoughts, where magic spreads.
Echoes linger, soft and clear,
A melody that draws us near.

With open hearts, we chase the sound,
In silent nights, where love is found.
Echoes ripple through the stars,
In every pulse, no bounds, no bars.

As we unite in cosmic grace,
The ethereal realm, our sacred space.
In echoes sweet, we find our way,
Together bound in night and day.

Journey Through the Veiled Silence

In stillness deep, the silence calls,
A journey vast, where darkness falls.
With open minds, and hearts aglow,
In veiled silence, we learn to grow.

The path of stars, it winds and weaves,
Through shadows cast by ancient leaves.
In every pause, the truth reveals,
A silent bond that gently heals.

As whispers dance on twilight's breath,
We tread with grace, defying death.
In veiled silence, we find our way,
Through dreams and hopes, we'll never stray.

Together bound, in sacred trust,
We journey on, as all things must.
Through veiled silence, love shall guide,
In harmony, we'll ever bide.

Between Light and Shade

In whispers soft, the shadows creep,
They dance with light, in secrets deep.
A fragile line, where dreams collide,
A gentle touch, where hearts abide.

The sun dips low, the sky ignites,
With hues of gold, it bids good nights.
The world stands still, as dusk unfolds,
Embracing stories yet untold.

Each beam of hope, each lingering gaze,
A balance struck in twilight's maze.
Where laughter flows, and sorrows wane,
Between light's kiss and shadows' reign.

In quiet moments, the truth laid bare,
A tapestry of dreams to share.
In this realm where contrasts play,
We find our peace, 'twixt light and shade.

Wraiths of the Dusk

Beneath the veil of twilight's gloom,
The shadows cast their silent doom.
Wraiths wander forth on whispered winds,
In search of solace, where night begins.

The stars awaken, the moon takes flight,
Illuminating the depths of night.
Figures flicker, like dying flames,
In haunting calls, they whisper names.

Echoes linger, the past remains,
In dreams we chase, through joy and pains.
A dance of ghosts, a spectral play,
Wraiths of the dusk, they find their way.

In these moments, we dare to see,
The shades of what could never be.
As twilight fades and dawn's light breaks,
The wraiths retreat, the heart awakes.

Silhouettes in the Haze

In the morning mist, where shadows blend,
Silhouettes rise, as dreams descend.
Figures unknown, yet deeply felt,
In this quiet space, our truths are dealt.

The world obscured by a soft embrace,
Unraveled stories, we dare to trace.
Silent whispers fill the air,
In hazy realms, we lay ourselves bare.

Each outline speaks in muted tones,
A realm where heart and spirit roams.
In the fading light, we search for grace,
Silhouettes in the haze, we find our place.

As daylight breaks, the mist retreats,
Revealing lives and chance encounters sweet.
Yet in that fog, we learned to dream,
In shadows whispering, we find our theme.

Veiled Perspectives

Through curtains drawn, a world concealed,
Veiled perspectives, fate revealed.
What we perceive is seldom truth,
In shifting sands of age and youth.

Glimmers hidden behind our eyes,
Each thought a spark, a soft disguise.
A tapestry woven with threads of doubt,
In tangled dreams, we twist about.

Sculpting visions from life's clay,
Minds adrift in the light of day.
As we ponder, reflect, and see,
Our veiled perspectives set us free.

For in the depths of thought we find,
A universe brimming, intertwined.
In shadows cast, and light so bold,
The stories of our lives unfold.

Chasing the Phantom

I run through shadows, swift and light,
Whispers of dreams, fading from sight.
A flicker of hope, a shadowy trace,
I chase the phantom, lost in the space.

The night brings secrets, veiled and deep,
Echoes of laughter, promises to keep.
With every step, I venture astray,
In search of the dawn, to light up the way.

Through forests of doubt, and rivers of fear,
I summon the strength, for you to draw near.
Yet as I reach out, you slip from my hand,
A fleeting illusion, on shimmering sand.

But I won't relent, this quest won't be done,
For even in shadows, the light can be spun.
I'll roam till the end, through night and through gleam,
In pursuit of the phantom, forever I dream.

Ethereal Shrouds

Veils of mist dance, in silvery night,
Soft whispers flutter, like birds in flight.
They cloak the world in a soft embrace,
Ethereal shrouds weave a tender grace.

Stars twinkle shyly, beyond the pale,
As dreams interlace, and memories sail.
Each step in the fog, a story untold,
Wrapped in the magic, of courage bold.

The moon bathes the earth, in a spectral glow,
While shadows unfold, where silence flows.
Each heartbeat echoes, a rhythmic sound,
In the arms of the night, where lost dreams are found.

With whispers of hope, the dawn shall arise,
Casting away fears, giving truth to the lies.
Yet for now, I linger, in the cool of this shroud,
Embraced by the beauty, wrapped in its cloud.

The Hidden Trail

Leaves rustle softly, beneath my feet,
Winding through valleys, where wildflowers meet.
A path untraveled, with secrets to share,
The hidden trail calls, through twilight's glare.

Beneath the tall trees, where shadows play,
I follow the whispers, that lead me away.
Each twist and turn, a new wonder unfolds,
Stories of yesteryear, waiting to be told.

The fragrance of pine, dances in the air,
With every heartbeat, revealing a prayer.
Embraced by stillness, my spirit feels free,
On this hidden trail, just nature and me.

Yet as I wander, I ponder the cost,
What is found here, and what might be lost?
For life is a journey, with paths intertwined,
The hidden trail beckons, to all who seek kind.

Drift of the Timeless

In the hush of the night, time seems to sway,
Moments drift softly, like clouds in the fray.
Each breath holds a story, of where we have been,
A dance of the timeless, where dreams weave in.

The stars spin their tales, in the canvas of sky,
Fleeting glimpses of sage, that leap and fly.
The river of ages, flows ceaselessly on,
Through echoes of laughter, and whispers of dawn.

Breathe deep of the silence, let it wrap tight,
In this drift of the timeless, we find our light.
For every heartbeat carries, a truth we must find,
In the drift of the timeless, we're one of a kind.

So let go of the worry, let go of the fight,
Embrace the unknown, hold your dreams tight.
In the drift of the timeless, together we roam,
Through the echoes of ages, we find our home.

Beyond the Gloom

In shadows deep where silence dwells,
A whisper calls, the heart compels.
With hope anew, we take the leap,
Beyond the gloom, our dreams to keep.

The stars align, in night they gleam,
A tapestry of every dream.
Through darkness vast, we find the light,
Beyond the gloom, we take our flight.

With every step, we shed our fear,
A brighter dawn will soon be near.
In unity, our spirits rise,
Beyond the gloom, we touch the skies.

So hand in hand, let's forge our way,
With faith and love, we'll brave the day.
The journey long, the path unclear,
Beyond the gloom, the future's here.

Lost in the Ether

In realms unseen, drift thoughts like mist,
Whispers of dreams, a longing twist.
Echoes dance in the silent air,
Lost in the ether, without a care.

The stars blink softly in vast embrace,
Each spark a story, a fleeting trace.
Time bends like light, so hard to see,
Lost in the ether, just you and me.

Moments linger, then slip away,
Like grains of sand at the close of day.
Yet in this space, our hearts shall soar,
Lost in the ether, forevermore.

We'll weave a world from threads of night,
In cosmic dance, we find our light.
Together we float, fearless and free,
Lost in the ether, just you and me.

Fading Shapes of the Past

Ghosts of memories gently fade,
In corners dark, where shadows played.
The laughter lingers, soft refrain,
Fading shapes of joy and pain.

Time's gentle hand erases the lines,
The echoes of love, like whispered signs.
Yet in the heart, they ever last,
Fading shapes of the cherished past.

Through photographs and quiet sighs,
We hold onto what never dies.
Those fleeting moments carved in stone,
Fading shapes, yet never alone.

Embrace the past, let it renew,
In whispers soft, it speaks to you.
In every heartbeat, shadows cast,
Fading shapes of the bonds we've amassed.

The Enchanted Veil

Beneath the stars, a wonder sprawls,
An enchanted veil that softly calls.
With every breath, a magic stirs,
In hushed tones, the secret purrs.

The moonlight weaves through ancient trees,
Safer than dreams, a gentle breeze.
In twilight's grip, the world unveils,
The hidden paths of the enchanted trails.

With every step on this sacred ground,
A harmony of lost and found.
In whispered words, our spirits sail,
Together lost in the enchanted veil.

So take my hand, let's wander through,
In realms of old, where dreams feel new.
Together we'll dance in the ethereal gale,
In love's embrace, the enchanted veil.

Milton Keynes UK
Ingram Content Group UK Ltd.
UKHW022050111124
451035UK00014B/1036